Barry the Bear & Billy the Bee

By: Jasmine Joseph

Illustrated by: Olga Ladyga

Barry the Bear and Billy the Bee

©2020 Jasmine Joseph

print ISBN: 978-1-09834-846-5

Barry the Bear
and Billy the Bee

By: Jasmine Joseph
Illustrated by: Olga Ladyga

Once upon a time, there was a bear and a bee.
Barry the Bear and Billy the Bee,
Two best friends, who always met under the
apple tree.

Billy was on his way to meet with Barry,
and Billy was having the best day ever!
Billy sees Barry under the apple tree,
so Billy goes and says hello.

"Hi Barry, how are you doing today?"
Barry looked up with tears in his eyes and
replied.
"Umm, I'm okay. I'm not having the best
day."
"What's the matter?" Says Billy.
Sadly, Barry replied, "I've lost my light."
Billy looked confused, "Your light?"

"Yes my grandfather gave it to me."
"Well where did you last have it?"
"I don't remember."
"Okay, I'll help you find it!"

"Will you Billy, will you really help me find it?"
"Of course, you're my best friend!"

So, Billy and Barry begin to search through the woods for Barry's light.
They searched under rocks, in trees, and over mountains.

They asked the birds and the flowers…

... the bees, the lions, the hippos,
even the porcupines,
and no one had seen Barry's light.

Barry and Billy started to get discouraged now, because the sun was starting to set, and they knew they'd have to be home soon.

So, they started to head back towards the apple tree. As they headed back, they continued to ask, look, and search, finding nothing.

Once they got to the apple tree, Barry plops down right in front of it and sighs. " I guess my light is gone forever." Billy says, "No Barry, we'll find it. We'll look tomorrow."
"It's no use Billy. We've looked everywhere."

As Barry says these words, the sun begins to set. As the sun sets, Barry's heart begins to glow. Billy notices Barry's heart is starting to light up and Billy says in all his excitement,

"Barry look, look you're glowing!"

"What, what, what do you mean Billy? What's going on?"

"Look Barry look, look at your heart!"

Billy says, "See Barry, your light was
in you the whole time.
Your light is always in you."
"I love you Billy."
"I love you Barry."
"Thank you."

Good night.